Little Elephant

Madison Parker

GROWING UP WILD

NORWOOD HOUSE PRESS

Cataloging-in-Publication Data

Names: Parker, Madison.
Title: Little elephants / Madison Parker.
Description: Buffalo, NY : Norwood House Press, 2026. | Series: Growing up wild | Includes glossary and index.
Identifiers: ISBN 9781978574113 (pbk.) | ISBN 9781978574120 (library bound) | ISBN 9781978574137 (ebook)
Subjects: LCSH: Elephants--Infancy--Juvenile literature. | Elephants--Juvenile literature.
Classification: LCC QL737.P98 P375 2026 | DDC 599.6713'92--dc23

Published in 2026 by
Norwood House Press
2544 Clinton Street
Buffalo, NY 14224

Designer: Rhea Magaro
Editor: Kim Thompson

Photo credits: Cover, p. 1 Romi Gamit/Shutterstock.com; p. 5 Johan Swanepoel/Shutterstock.com; p. 6 Alonephotoshoot/Shutterstock.com; p. 7 Zhukova Valentyna/Shutterstock.com; pp. 8, 9 Saranga/Shutterstock.com; p. 10 MFadly29/Shutterstock.com; p. 11 yudachen/Shutterstock.com; p. 13 Diane Sisku/Shutterstock.com; p. 14 gypsy.giko/Shutterstock.com; p. 15 Galyna Andrushk/Shutterstock.como; p. 17 Michelle Guillermin/Shutterstock.com; p. 18 Dawid Fourie Photography/Shutterstock.com; p. 19 Klipkins; p. 21 Jane Rix/Shutterstock.com;

Printed in the United States of America

CPSIA compliance information: Batch #CSNHP26: For further information contact Norwood House Press at 1-800-237-9932.

TABLE OF CONTENTS

Little Elephants

Elephants grow up in the **wild**. Baby elephants are called calves.

How Baby Elephants Look

Elephant calves are big! They have big ears.

They have long **trunks**. Their small **tusks** will grow bigger.

Baby elephants are born with hair. The hair keeps them cool. It moves heat away from their bodies.

How Baby Elephants Sound

Baby elephants use sounds to **communicate**.

They **trumpet** when they are excited.

They roar when they are angry.

What Baby Elephants Eat

Calves drink milk from their mothers. They try other foods when they are about six months old.

Elephants are **herbivores**.

They eat plants.

As they grow, baby elephants eat leaves and **twigs**. They eat grass and fruit.

Lots to Learn

Baby elephants live with a **herd**. They learn from other elephants. They learn to **forage** for food.

When they are eight months old, calves practice using their trunks.

They use their trunks to eat and drink.
They use their trunks to take baths!

All Grown Up

Teenage elephants are **mature**. Females stay with the herd. Males leave to find new homes.

Glossary

communicate (kuh-MYOO-ni-kate): to share information and feelings

forage (FOR-ij): to search for food

herbivores (HUR-buh-vorz): animals that eat only plants

herd (hurd): a group of animals that live and move together

mature (muh-CHOOR): fully grown or developed; adult

trumpet (TRUHM-pit): to make a loud, musical sound

trunks (truhngks): the long, flexible noses of elephants that are used for many purposes

tusks (tuhsks): long, pointed teeth that grow outside of an elephant's mouth

twigs (twigs): small, thin branches from a tree or bush

wild (wilde): natural places where no people live

Thinking Questions

1. What are baby elephants called?

2. Name three body parts that elephants have.

3. How do herds help baby elephants?

4. What do baby elephants eat?

5. How do baby elephants use their trunks?

Index

About the Author

Madison Parker spent her childhood in the city of Chicago, Illinois. A farm girl at heart, today she lives in Wisconsin with her husband and four children on a small farm with cows, goats, chickens, and two miniature horses named Harley and David. Her favorite dessert is vanilla frozen custard with rainbow sprinkles, even in the winter.